Facts About
Energy
All Around Us

DONNA BAILEY

RSVP
RAINTREE
STECK-VAUGHN
P U B L I S H E R S
The Steck-Vaughn Company

Austin, Texas

How to Use This Book

This book tells you many things about energy and how we move it. There is a Table of Contents on the next page. It shows you what each double page of the book is about. For example, pages 8 and 9 tell you about "Oil and Gas by Pipeline."

On most of these pages you will find some words that are printed in **bold** type. The bold type shows you that these words are in the Glossary on pages 46 and 47. The Glossary explains the meaning of some words that may be new to you.

At the very end of the book there is an Index. The Index tells you where to find certain words in the book. For example, you can use it to look up words like substation, electrons, and circuit, and many other words to do with moving energy.

Library of Congress Cataloging-in-Publication Data

Bailey, Donna.
  Energy all around us / written by Donna Bailey.
    p. cm. — (Facts about)
  Includes index.
  Summary: Discusses different kinds of energy, where it comes from, how it is stored and transported, and how it is used.
  ISBN 0-8114-2520-7
  1. Power resource—Juvenile literature. [1. Power resources.]
I. Title. II. Series: Facts about (Austin, Tex.)
TJ163.23.B35 1991   90-39294
333.79—dc20   CIP AC

Printed and bound in the United States of America
2 3 4 5 6 7 8 9 0 LB 95 94 93

Contents

Introduction

People, animals, plants, and machines
all use **energy** to move or to work.
The energy comes from different sources,
like oil, coal, and sunshine. We have
learned how to turn some kinds of energy
into **electricity.**

This book tells us how we store energy
and move it around by road and rail,
by pipeline or along wires.

Machines move because they get energy by burning fuel like oil or coal. People get energy from the food they eat.

In some places, people do not have many machines on their farms. They use their own energy to dig the soil.

Sometimes they use animals to help carry heavy loads.

when we eat hamburgers our bodies use the energy stored in the meat and the bun

Where Energy Comes From

Sun's rays

Sun

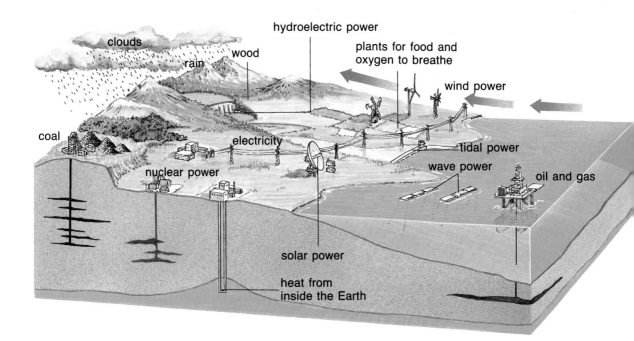

clouds
rain
wood
hydroelectric power
plants for food and
oxygen to breathe
wind power
coal
electricity
tidal power
nuclear power
wave power
oil and gas
solar power
heat from
inside the Earth

The energy from the Sun is
called **radiant energy.**
This energy gives us **solar power.**
Heat and light from the Sun travel as
rays which help to make plants grow.

After millions of years dead plants
in the rocks turn into **fossil fuels**
such as coal, oil, and natural gas.

We can make electricity by using the
energy in moving wind and water and
the energy stored in **nuclear power.**

6

you can see energy in a flash of lightning

A flash of lightning is a huge amount of electrical energy leaping from one cloud to another. When the wind bends the trees, its power and energy can break the branches. The tides and the waves that pound the coast during a storm hold great power. In some countries hot rocks buried deep in the Earth give out **geothermal energy.**

Energy is all around us and we have to find the best ways to use it.

Oil and Gas by Pipeline

laying an underground pipeline

Oil and natural gas are often found in the desert. From there they are pumped along a pipeline to a **gas plant** or **oil refinery.**

Then they are changed into products like bottled gas or gasoline.

8

Sometimes engineers dig a huge trench to bury the pipeline. However, pipelines cannot be buried in very cold places inside the Arctic Circle. The heat of the oil would melt the frozen earth.

the Trans-Alaskan pipeline is raised above the ground

divers help guide a pipeline into position

It is more difficult to lay a pipeline under the sea. Lengths of pipe are welded together on board a ship. Cranes lower the pipeline to the seabed from a barge.

laying a pipeline at sea

Oil and Gas
by Tanker

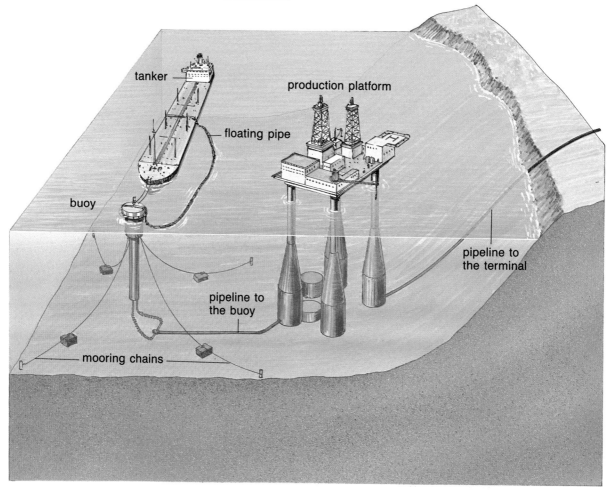

tanker

production platform

floating pipe

buoy

pipeline to
the terminal

pipeline to
the buoy

mooring chains

Some undersea pipelines carry oil and
natural gas to the nearest port.
Then ships take them to a refinery.

Oil from a **production platform** is
loaded onto huge ships called tankers.
The tankers tie up to a buoy and the
oil is loaded through a floating pipe.

Very large tankers called supertankers carry as much as 500,000 tons of oil. Supertankers need very deep water to load and unload. When they want to unload the oil, they tie up to a **single buoy mooring** anchored in deep water off the shore. The oil is pumped from the holds of the tanker along a floating pipeline to storage tanks on the shore.

a tanker tied up to a buoy

Gas is more difficult than oil to carry because it takes up more space. The gas is cooled to −256°F and becomes liquid. Liquified natural gas or LNG is carried on special ships.

LNG must be kept cold, so it is carried in special tanks on the ship

Refining Oil

Crude oil from a well is changed into different products at an oil refinery. The oil is heated to 660° F in the boiler house and then it is pumped into a tall **fractionating tower.** Here the **hydrocarbons** separate out at different temperatures to make many different oil products.

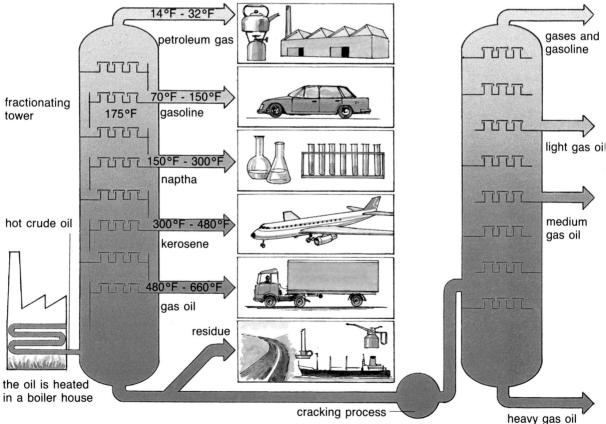

14°F - 32°F

petroleum gas

fractionating tower

70°F - 150°F

175°F   gasoline

150°F - 300°F

naptha

hot crude oil

300°F - 480°F

kerosene

480°F - 660°F

gas oil

residue

the oil is heated in a boiler house

cracking process

gases and gasoline

light gas oil

medium gas oil

heavy gas oil

12

an oil refinery in the Netherlands

The tiniest part of everything in the world is called an **atom.** A hydrocarbon **molecule** is made when a **hydrogen** atom joins to a **carbon** atom.

Scientists can change less useful oil products into more useful products by cracking or splitting chains of molecules. The molecules change shape when they are heated to very high temperatures.

Chains of molecules can be shortened, or branches can be added to them.

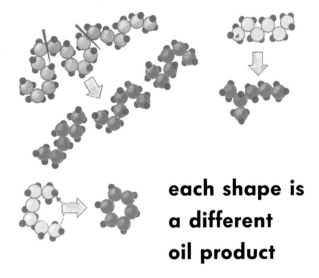

each shape is a different oil product

Loops of molecules can be closed to make a circle.

13

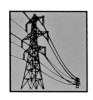

Moving Gasoline

Cars, trucks, airplanes, and trains burn
a lot of fuel every day. Most of this
fuel is gasoline, diesel oil, or aviation fuel.
Pipelines take fuel to the largest
users, such as railroads and airports.

In Australia huge trucks called "road
trains" carry gasoline from the refinery
at Darwin to storage places or depots.

Most car drivers get their gasoline or diesel oil from pumps at filling stations. Road tankers take the fuel from the refinery to the filling stations and pump it into underground storage tanks.

Long-distance truck drivers have to know where they can buy extra fuel.

a desert filling station in Algeria

Large amounts of gasoline can be carried for long distances by railroads in special tank cars.

Moving Coal

Coal is often used to make electricity.
  The coal is loaded from storage towers
at the coal mine into railroad cars
and carried directly to a power station.
The track leads into the **hopper house.**
Doors in the bottom of the wagons open.
The coal falls into the hoppers below.
The doors close and the empty train
circles back to the power station.

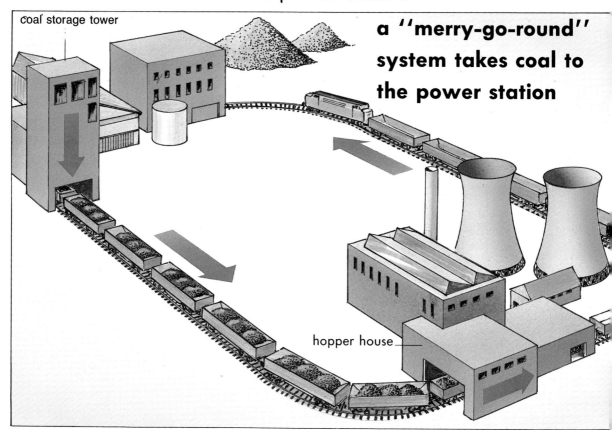

coal storage tower

a ''merry-go-round'' system takes coal to the power station

hopper house

trains take coal from this mine 375 miles to the sea

Because coal is heavy, dirty, and takes up a lot of space, it is difficult to move. Conveyor belts carry coal from mines to power stations or nearby ports.

Trains also carry coal from mines to the coast to be loaded onto ships.

conveyor belts load coal onto a ship in Australia

Atoms and Electricity

Scientists studying atoms through a microscope found out that every atom has a **nucleus** in the middle. **Electrons** travel around the nucleus, just as the Earth travels around the Sun. Each nucleus has the same number of **neutrons** and **protons** clinging together.

Electrons have a **negative charge** and attract protons with a **positive charge.**

The black holes in the photograph show the atoms that make up a metal called **tungsten.** The photograph was taken through a very powerful **microscope** which makes the piece of tungsten three million times larger than its real size.

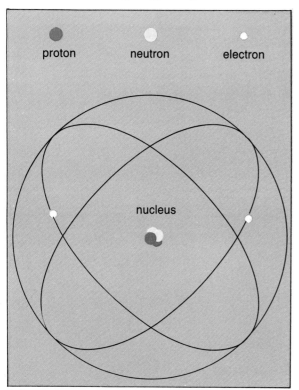

proton　　neutron　　electron

nucleus

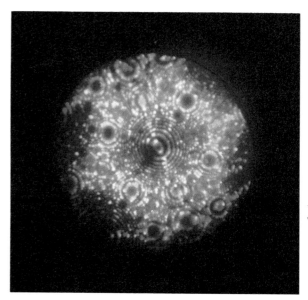

In 1752 Benjamin Franklin risked his life to fly a kite in a thunderstorm. A flash of lightning charged a metal key on the kite with electricity. This proved that lightning is electricity.

Electrons from a thunder cloud are attracted to positive charges on the ground and jump the gap, making the lightning.

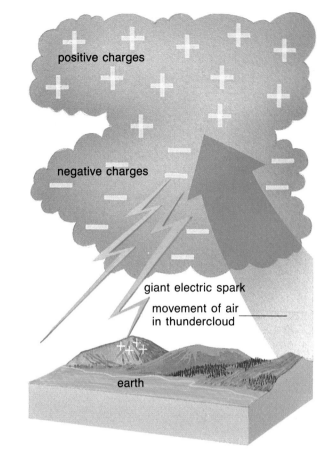

positive charges

negative charges

giant electric spark

movement of air in thundercloud

earth

How a Battery Works

Electricity stored in a battery
is static electricity which does not move.
An electric current is a stream of
electrons moving through a wire.

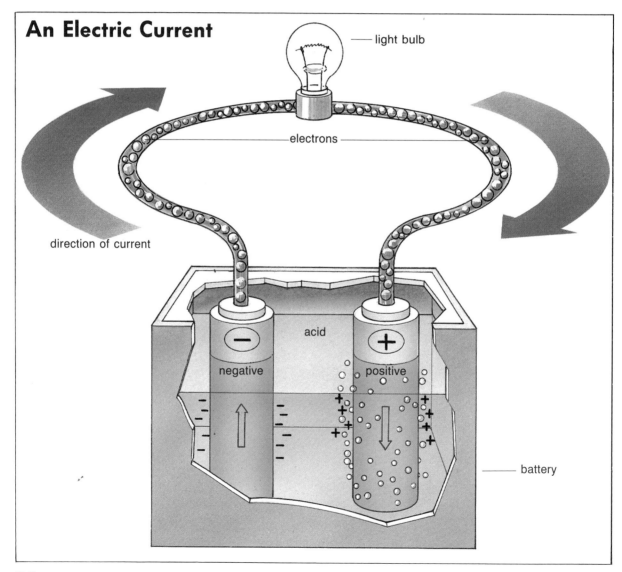

An Electric Current

light bulb

electrons

direction of current

acid

− negative

+ positive

battery

Alessandro Volta was the first person to make an electric battery using different metals in a bath of **acid.** He caused a **chemical reaction** which released streams of electrons to make positive and negative charges.

When a wire joins a positive charge to a negative charge it makes a **circuit** and the electrons move along the wire. Electrons have a negative charge so they are attracted to the positive end of the battery.

The electrons keep moving around the circuit and can light a bulb unless a switch cuts them off.

Volta shows how his battery works

Making Electric Current

In 1819 Hans Oersted found a link between electricity and magnetism. He put a wire carrying an electric current near a magnet. The magnet turned toward the wire.

In 1831 Michael Faraday discovered that if he pushed a magnet in and out of a coil of wire he could make an electric current flow through the wire. We still use this method today to make electricity for electric motors.

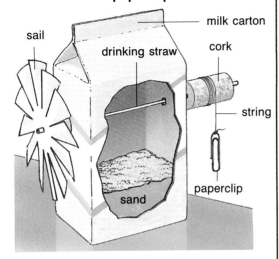

sail

milk carton

drinking straw

cork

string

paperclip

sand

Alternating current flows first in one direction and then in the other.

In most electric motors the magnet stands still and the **electromagnet** carrying the alternating current moves.

The diagram shows how a simple electric motor works. When the current is switched on, the wire loop turns half a circle in one direction and then in the opposite direction when the current switches its **poles** from north to south or from south to north.

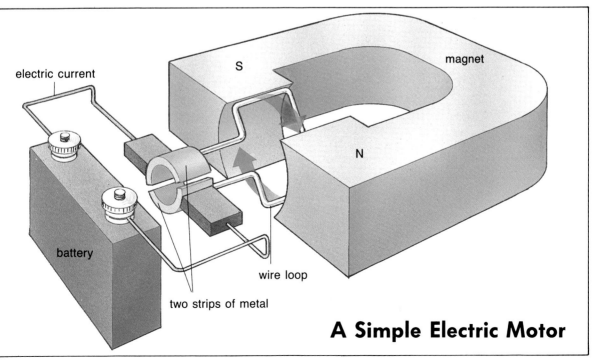

electric current

magnet

S

N

battery

wire loop

two strips of metal

A Simple Electric Motor

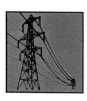

Pipelines and Sea Routes

The map shows where coal, oil, and natural gas are moved around the world.

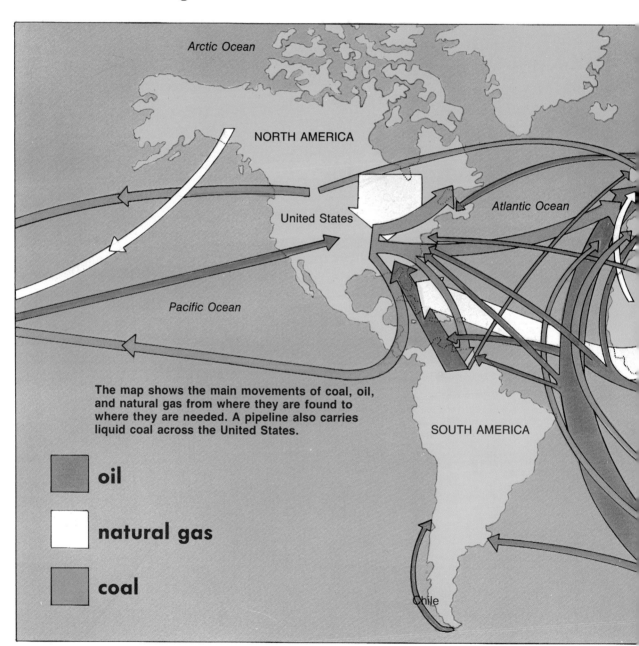

Arctic Ocean

NORTH AMERICA

United States

Atlantic Ocean

Pacific Ocean

The map shows the main movements of coal, oil, and natural gas from where they are found to where they are needed. A pipeline also carries liquid coal across the United States.

SOUTH AMERICA

Chile

oil

natural gas

coal

Oil from the Middle East goes by tanker
to Europe and Japan. In addition,
Japan buys coal from the United
States and Australia and natural gas
from the North American gas fields.

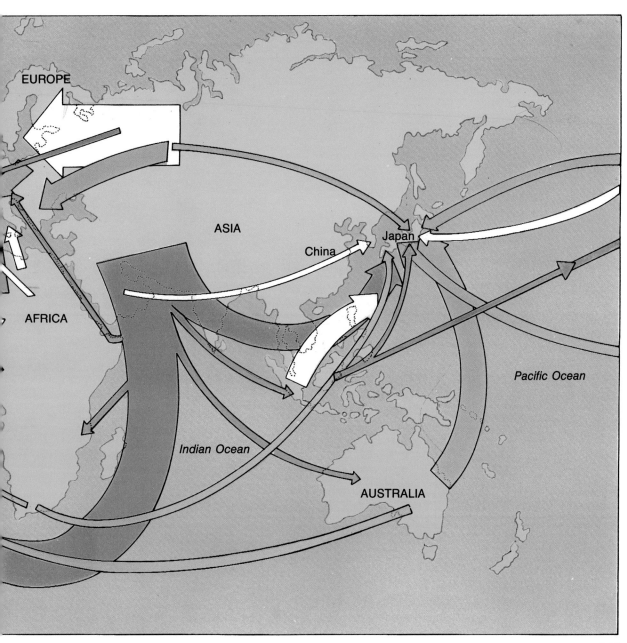

Power Stations

Thomas Edison built the world's first
power station in New York in 1881.

Most power stations work by heating
water until it turns into steam.
The steam turns the blades of **turbines,**
which turn wheels connected to the huge
electromagnets inside the **generators.**
The generators change the **mechanical
energy** of the turbines into electrical
energy.

Some power stations burn coal, oil, or gas to make steam to turn the turbines. At **hydroelectric power** stations, fast-flowing water spins the turbines.

A nuclear power station uses the energy from splitting atoms of **uranium.** Just one speck of uranium can generate enough electricity to boil hundreds of pots of water.

Carrying Electricity

Power lines or thick wires called
cables carry electricity from the power
stations to the customers. The wires
are bound tightly together inside a
tough covering. Many countries link
the power lines to make a huge supply
system called a **grid.**

Tall steel pylons hold up the cables
across the countryside. Pylons take up too
much room in towns so cables there are
buried underground.

A fault in the system that carries
electricity can cause problems.
The engineers who look after the
overhead lines have to repair faults.

**engineers
work high
above the
ground to
repair faults
in the cables**

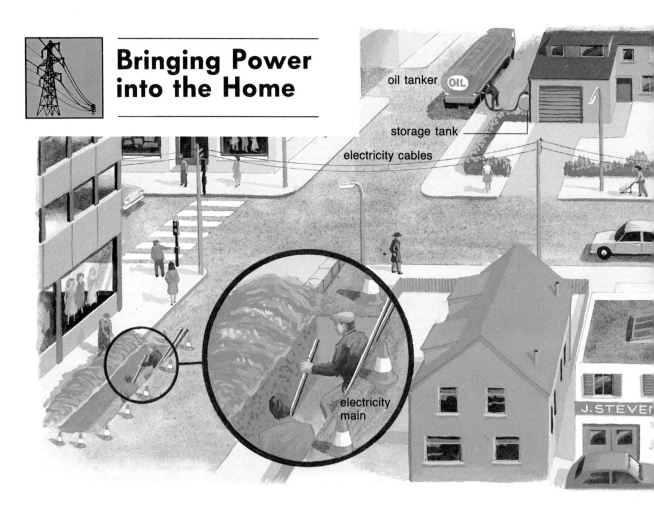

Bringing Power into the Home

oil tanker OIL

storage tank

electricity cables

electricity main

J. STEVE[N]

Most homes in a town are supplied with gas from a gas pipeline and electricity from an electricity cable.

Most of the pipes and cables are buried underground below the roads so you can only see them when workers dig them up. In some places you can see overhead electricity cables carried on poles. Some people use coal, oil, wood, or bottled gas for heating and cooking.

gas main

place to store coal

bottled gas

coal

wood

Power companies sell gas and electricity to people. **Meters** measure how much electricity people use. Some people make their own electricity using an oil-fired generator or a windmill.

a windmill in Malta

How Lights Work

When you put on a light switch, a spring pushes the electrical **contacts** together. The circuit is now complete and electrons can flow along the wire into the glass bulb. Inside the bulb the electrons flow along a very thin piece of tungsten wire called a **filament** which becomes white hot and glows with a bright light.

When you turn the switch off, the contacts separate and electricity cannot flow.

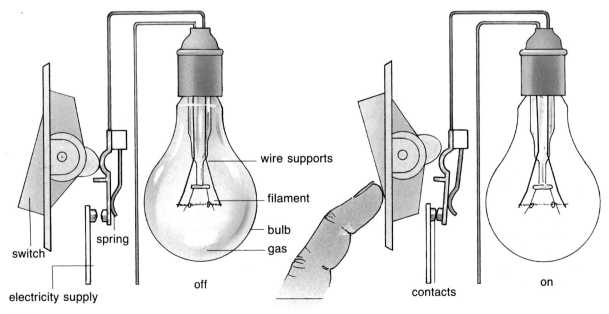

switch

electricity supply

spring

off

wire supports

filament

bulb

gas

contacts

on

32

car headlights and street lamps light up New York at night

We often use **fluorescent lights** in schools, shops, offices, and streets. A fluorescent light uses less electrical current than an ordinary lamp bulb. It has a glass tube which contains a small drop of **mercury** vapor or gas. The electrons flow along the tube and make the gas send out rays of light. These rays hit the sides of the tube, which are painted with a special paint that makes the tube glow brightly.

33

Measuring Electricity

Engineers measure the flow of
electrical current in **volts.**
The number of volts tells them the
pressure, or voltage, that makes the
electrons move along a wire.

The picture shows engineers testing
for faults on high voltage cables.

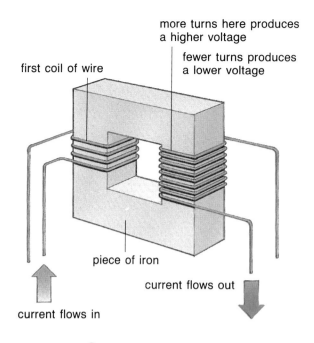

first coil of wire

more turns here produces a higher voltage

fewer turns produces a lower voltage

piece of iron

current flows out

current flows in

a transformer

a substation

Power stations generate electricity at very high voltage. The voltage is made even greater by **transformers** before the current is carried away on cables.

High voltage electricity can be carried along thick cables between pylons. The voltage is reduced at a **substation** before the electricity is used in offices, schools, and homes.

Using Electricity

We use electricity in many different ways in our homes and work places. Electric motors make machines turn. We use electricity to keep warm in winter and cool in summer, to give us light to see and heat to cook with. Many kitchens like the one in the picture are full of electrical things.

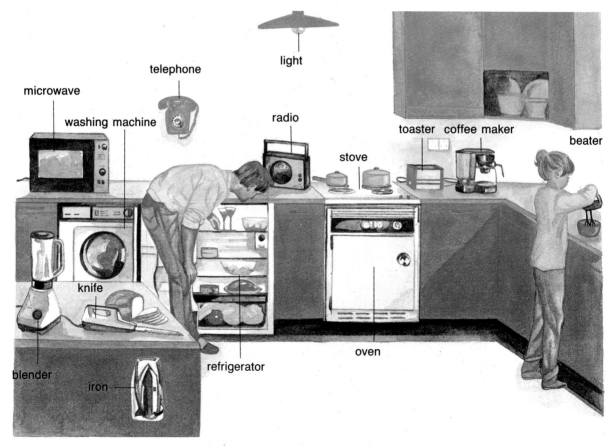

light

telephone

microwave

washing machine

radio

toaster   coffee maker

beater

stove

knife

blender

iron

refrigerator

oven

Farmers use electricity on their farms.
If the power is cut, a dairy farmer
may have to milk 100 cows by hand.

In many factories work is done by
electrical machines. The robots making
cars in this picture are powered
by electricity.

Keeping Energy Safe

The waste from nuclear power stations
is very little but it is very dangerous.
Trains carrying nuclear waste are kept
away from other traffic. The waste is
put into special strong containers,
like the third wagon from the front
on the train in the picture.

Wires carrying electricity are
insulated to stop people who touch them
from getting **electric shocks.**

Natural gas catches fire easily and may cause an explosion, so a smell is added to the gas at the gas plant. We can smell the gas if there is a leak.

If a pipeline or tanker is damaged the leaking oil will kill all the wildlife. Oil tankers like the one in the picture sometimes catch fire and burn for days.

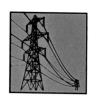

Running Out of Energy

Today we are using up fossil fuels very quickly because they are so useful.

The larger pictures show the amount of each fossil fuel left in the world. The smaller pictures show how much of each fuel we use up every year.

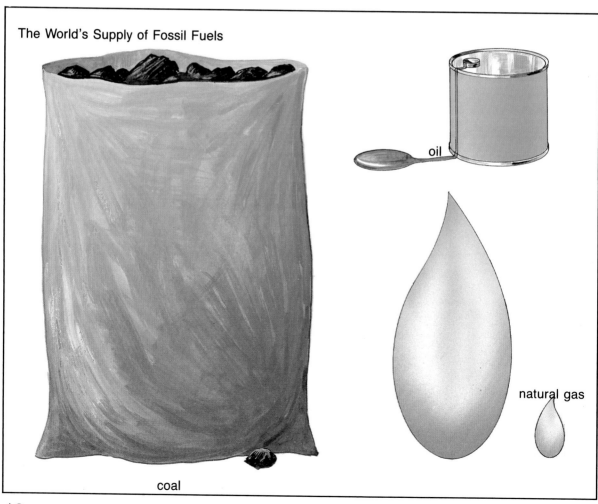

The World's Supply of Fossil Fuels

oil

natural gas

coal

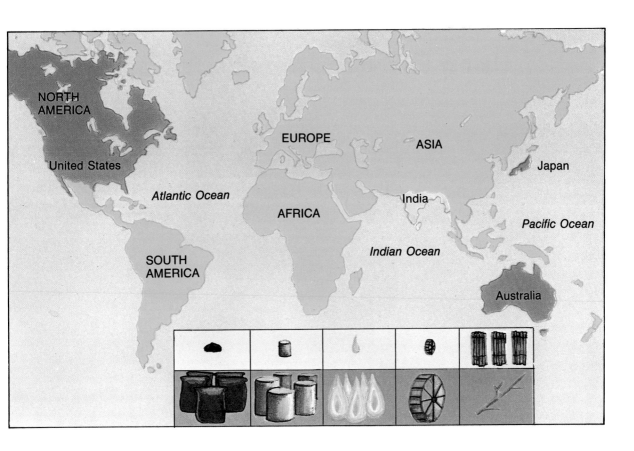

People think there is enough coal to
last for another 300 years. Gas may
last 60 years, but there may only
be oil for the next 35 years.

Nearly one-third of all the world's
energy is used in the United States.
Far more people live in India than in
the United States, but they only use a
tiny amount of the world's energy.
The table shows how much energy Indians
use compared to the people of North
America, Australia, and Japan.

Using Energy Carefully

The kind of power station shown in the
picture wastes huge amounts of energy.
Oil, gas, or coal must first be brought
long distances to the power station
before electricity can be generated.
Then the electricity must be taken away
to where it is needed in homes and factories.
All of this transportation is expensive and
wastes energy.

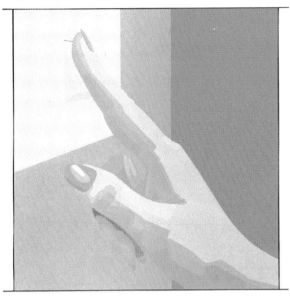

SWITCH OFF

UNWANTED LIGHTS

Saving energy by turning off lights is one way of making the world's sources of energy last longer.

The picture shows how we can save energy.
If we save paper, bottles, and cans, they could be **recycled** and used again. Garbage could even be used as a source of energy. When huge amounts are burned, enough heat is made to make electricity.

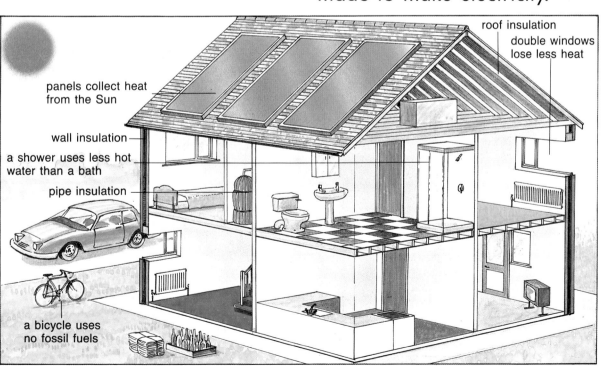

roof insulation
double windows lose less heat

panels collect heat from the Sun

wall insulation

a shower uses less hot water than a bath

pipe insulation

a bicycle uses no fossil fuels

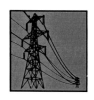

Energy and the Future

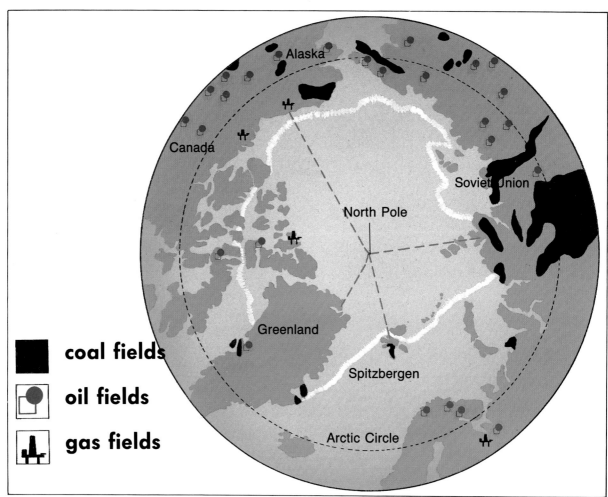

coal fields

oil fields

gas fields

Alaska

Canada

Soviet Union

North Pole

Greenland

Spitzbergen

Arctic Circle

There are huge oil fields under the
Arctic ice cap. Scientists think that
if they could build special roads
over the ice the oil could be carried
to Alaska, the Soviet Union,
and northern Europe.

Heat from the Sun can also be used as a source of energy. Scientists are trying to find ways of storing the Sun's energy for future use. In New Mexico, gas is heated by solar power and piped to buildings where it is used to make electricity. The cool gas then returns to be heated and used again.

Engineers are thinking of building power stations out at sea. They could take the gas directly from a gas field and turn it into electricity. They would not need to transport the gas first in tankers and pipelines.

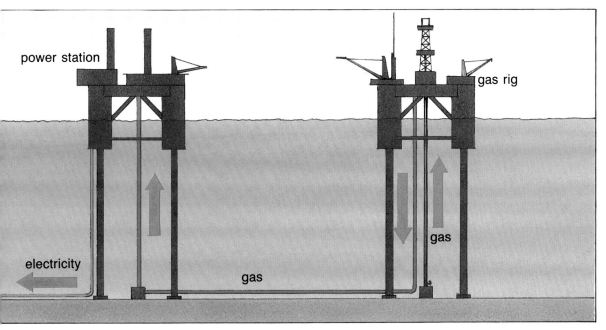

Glossary

acid   a strong liquid that can even dissolve metal.

atom   the smallest part of anything.

chemical reaction   the change that happens when two substances are joined.

circuit   the complete path of an electrical current.

contact   a point where one thing touches another.

crude oil   oil as it comes out of the ground.

electric shock   a tingling feeling you get from touching electric current. Electric shocks can be very dangerous.

electricity   a kind of energy or power used in homes and factories.

electromagnet   an iron bar with a coil of wire around it. The bar acts like a magnet when an electric current is passed through it.

electron   a part of an atom. It has a negative charge.

energy   the power to do work.

filament   a very fine thread, usually made of wire.

fluorescent light   a bright light made by ultraviolet rays.

fossil fuels   materials like oil, coal, and gas that were made by the remains of animals and plants millions of years ago.

fractionating tower   a tall tower used in processing crude oil. Different products are collected at each level.

gas plant   a place where a smell is added to natural gas.

generator   a machine for changing mechanical energy into electrical energy.

geothermal energy   power that is produced using heat from below the Earth's surface.

grid   the network that links all the power lines together.

hopper house   a building with large storage chambers in the shape of funnels.

hydrocarbon   a chemical mixture of hydrogen and carbon found in coal, oil, and natural gas.

hydroelectric power   electricity made by using fast-flowing water to drive a turbine.

hydrogen   a gas that is very light and burns easily.

insulated   covered with a material to stop electricity from passing through.

mechanical energy energy made by a machine.

mercury a silvery liquid metal.

meter an instrument for measuring or counting.

microscope an instrument for making things look larger.

molecule the smallest part of a mixture of chemicals. A molecule has at least two atoms.

negative charge the electrical charge of an electron. It pushes away other electrons.

neutron a part of an atom. It has no charge.

nuclear power energy produced when atoms are split.

nucleus the center of an atom.

oil refinery a factory that separates petroleum into a number of different fuels and chemicals.

oxygen a gas found in air and water. Plants and animals need oxygen to breathe.

pole either of the two ends of a magnet.

positive charge the electrical charge carried by a proton. It pushes away other protons.

production platform a large platform above sea level holding an oil rig and drill.

proton a part of an atom. It has a positive charge.

radiant energy a kind of energy that is given out in waves, or rays from a specific place, like a fire or the Sun.

recycle to reuse waste matter.

single buoy mooring a place for supertankers to tie up to. The mooring is in deep water off the coast and linked to the land by a pipeline.

solar power power from the Sun's rays which can be used to make electricity.

substation where high voltage electricity is reduced before the current is passed on.

transformer a machine that changes the force of an electric current.

tungsten a metal with a very high melting point.

turbine a wheel that has many curved blades. It is spun around rapidly by the movement of gas or a liquid.

uranium a metal used in nuclear power stations to make energy.

volt a unit of measurement of electricity.

Index

Photographic credits
(t = top b = bottom l = left r = right)
cover: Science Photo Library. Simon Fraser: **title page:** Science Photo Library, David Parker 5t Chris Fairclough Picture Library; 5b The Hutchison Library; 7 ZEFA; 8t The Hutchinson Library; 8b ZEFA; 9t Dick Clarke Seaphot; 9b Shell; 11/Hugh Jones Seaphot; 11r British Petroleum; 13, 14 15t Shell; 15b The Hutchison Library; 17t ZEFA; 17b Shell; 18 Science Photo Library; 21 Mansell Collection; 27 Science Photo Library; 28, 29 Central Electricity Generating Board; 31 David George Seaphot; 33 ZEFA; 34, 35 Central Electricity Generating Board; 37 Chris Fairclough Picture Library; 38 Science Photo Library; 39 ZEFA; 42 Science Photo Library; 43t Her Majesty's Stationery Office